Seasons

by E. Russell Primm III • illustrated by Kathleen Petelinsek

childsworld.com

Published by The Child's World®
800-599-READ • childsworld.com

Photography Credits
Creative Travel Projects/Shutterstock.com, cover; LedyX/Shutterstock.com, 1, 8; SZakharov/Shutterstock.com, 3; S_Photo/Shutterstock.com, 4; IM_photo/Shutterstock.com, 5; Flystock/Shutterstock.com, 6; Lucky Business/Shutterstock.com, 7; Oldrich/Shutterstock.com, 9; Wolkenengel565/Shutterstock.com, 10; TORWAISTUDIO/Shutterstock.com, 11; photolin/Shutterstock.com, 12; salajean/Shutterstock.com, 13; Bk87/Shutterstock.com, 14; Sean Xu/Shutterstock.com, 15; LightField Studios/Shutterstock.com, 16; Atsushi Hirao/Shutterstock.com, 17; sun ok/Shutterstock.com, 18; Stramp/Shutterstock.com, 19; Stuart Monk/Shutterstock.com, 20; myphotobank.com.au/Shutterstock.com, 21

ISBN Information
9781503889064 (Reinforced Library Binding)
9781503890145 (Portable Document Format)
9781503891388 (Online Multi-user eBook)
9781503892620 (Electronic Publication)

LCCN 2023950256

Printed in the United States of America

Note to Parents, Caregivers, and Educators:
The understanding of any language begins with the acquisition of vocabulary, whether the language is spoken or manual. The books in this series provide readers, both young and old, with basic American Sign Language signs. Combining close photo cues and simple, but detailed, line illustrations, children and adults alike can begin the process of learning American Sign Language.

Let these books be an introduction to the world of American Sign Language. Most languages have regional dialects and multiple ways of expressing the same thought. This is also true for sign language. We have attempted to use the most common version of the signs for the words in this series. As with any language, the best way to learn is to be taught in person by a frequent user. It is our hope that this series will pique your interest in sign language.

A special thanks to our advisers: As a member of a deaf family that spans four generations, **Kim Bianco Majeri** lives, works, and plays among the Deaf community. **Carmine L. Vozzolo** is an educator of children who are deaf and hard of hearing, as well as their families.

E. Russell Primm III was a well-known figure in the publishing industry who produced thousands of acclaimed books for children. He was affiliated with organizations such as the American Library Association, the Chicago Book Clinic, and the University of Chicago Publishing Program Advisory Board.

Kathleen Petelinsek has loved books since she was a child. Through the years, she has written, designed, and illustrated many books for children. She lives in Wisconsin, near her granddaughter who also shares her love for books.

Antarctica is the coldest place on Earth.

Winter

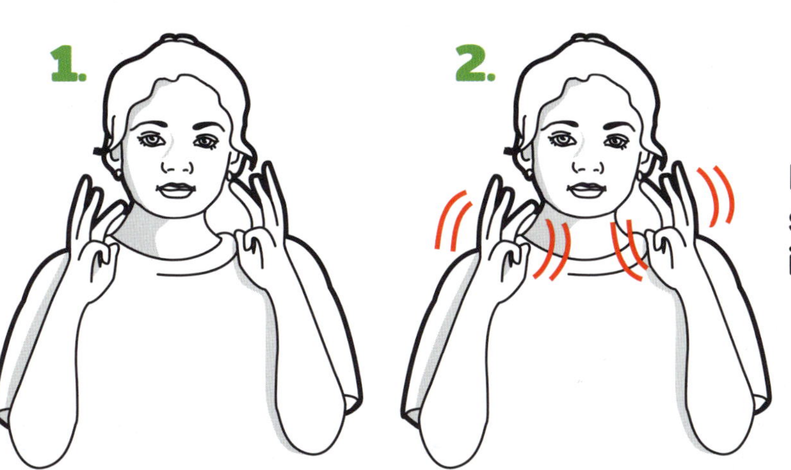

Make the "W" sign and shiver as if you are cold.

No two snowflakes are the same.

Snow

Wiggle all your fingers while moving your hands downward.

Snowboarding is a combination of skiing and skateboarding.

Snowboard

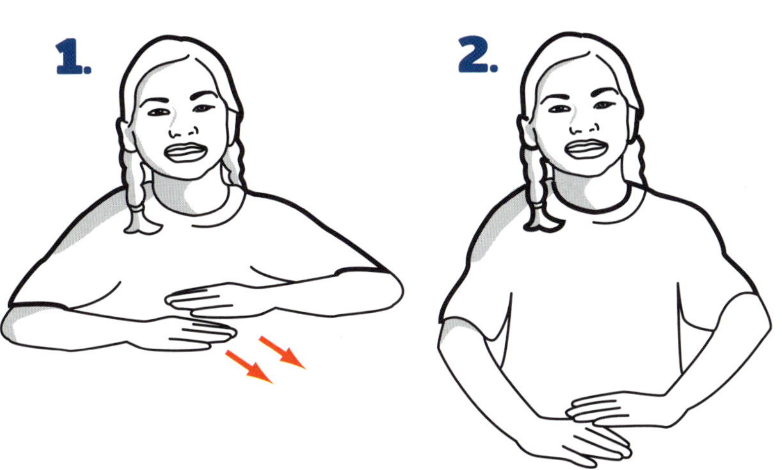

Both hands face down and slightly slice the air a few times.

Ice-skating takes a lot of practice.

Ice-Skate

Make the "X" sign. Move your arms back and forth in front of you.

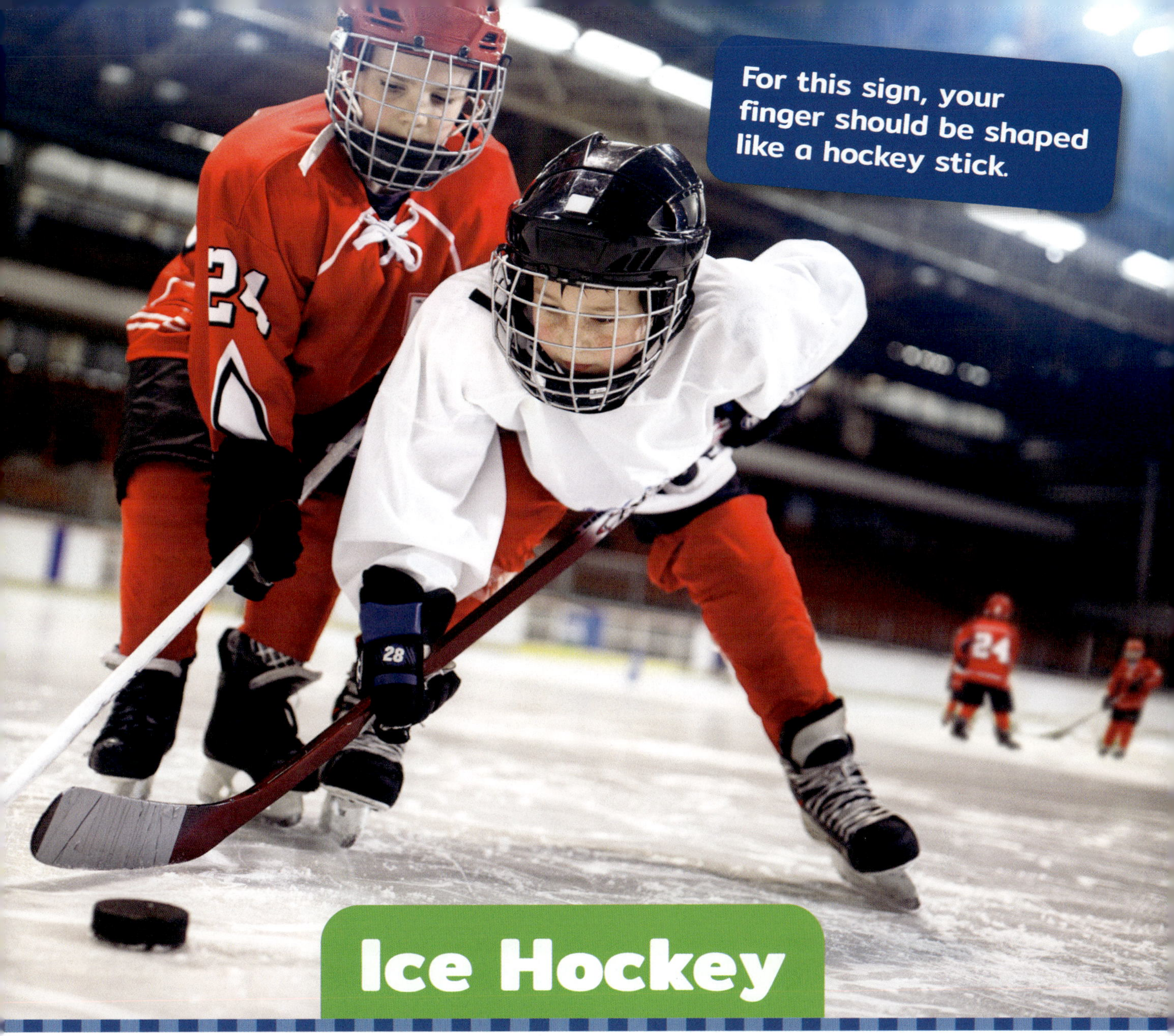

For this sign, your finger should be shaped like a hockey stick.

Ice Hockey

Make the "X" sign. Move it across your flat hand twice.

Many people say spring is their favorite season.

Spring

Put one hand around the other. Push up like a flower blooming.

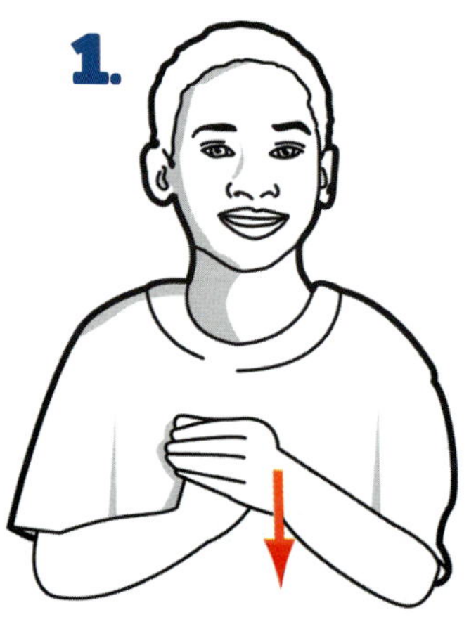

Birds make nests from twigs, mud, and even fabric.

Bird Nest

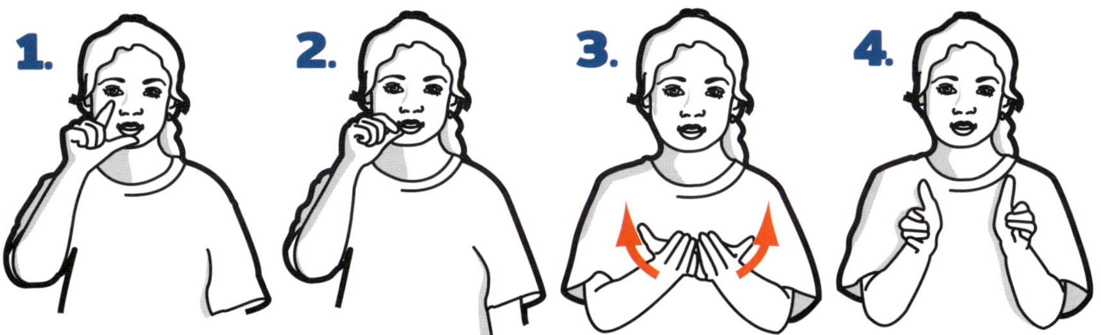

Make the sign for "bird" by making a beak with two fingers. Open and shut twice. Then make a bowl motion with your hands.

Don't wiggle your fingers for this sign—that would mean "snow."

Rain

Slightly curve your hands and move them downward. Repeat.

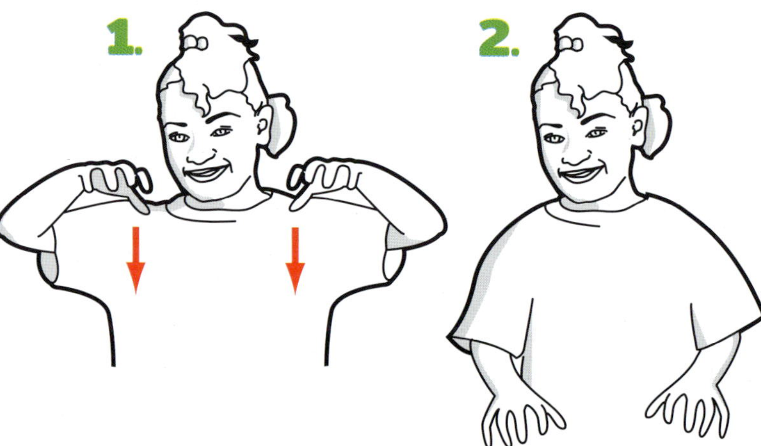

An umbrella is sometimes called a "parasol."

Umbrella

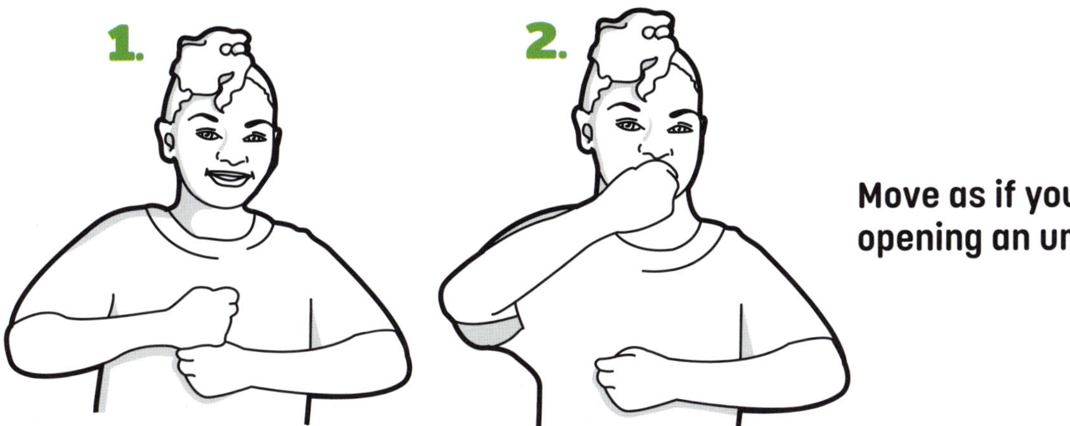

Move as if you are opening an umbrella.

Summer is the hottest season.

Summer

Move your right index finger from left to right across your forehead. Curl your finger when it reaches the right side.

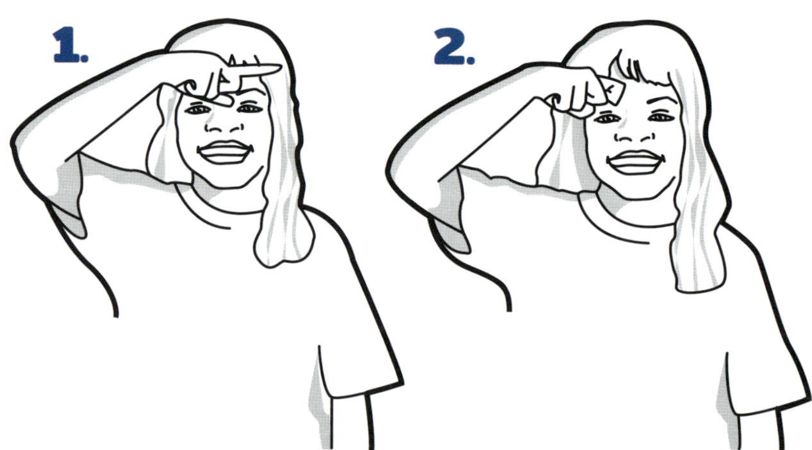

Some types of sunflowers can grow as tall as 15 feet (4.6 m)!

Sunflower

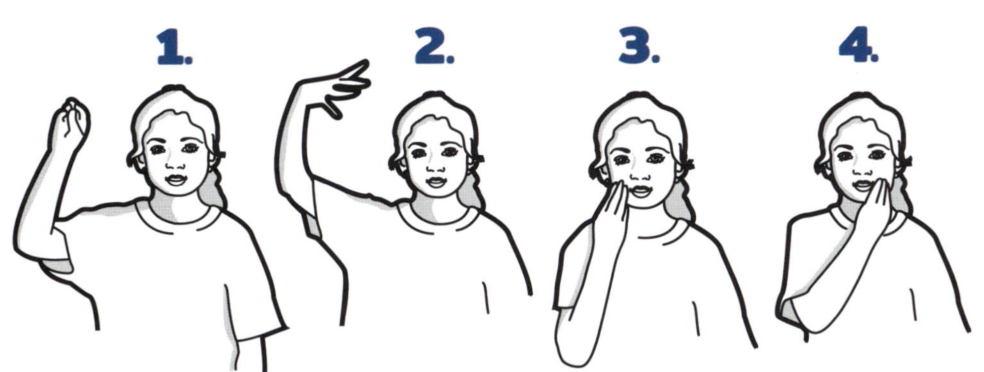

Pinch your fingers together. Make a small circle-motion with your hand, and "shine" on your head (like the sun). Then touch your pinched hand to one side of your nose, then the other.

Honeybees help plants grow.

Bee

Pretend to be stung on the cheek. Then swat the bee away.

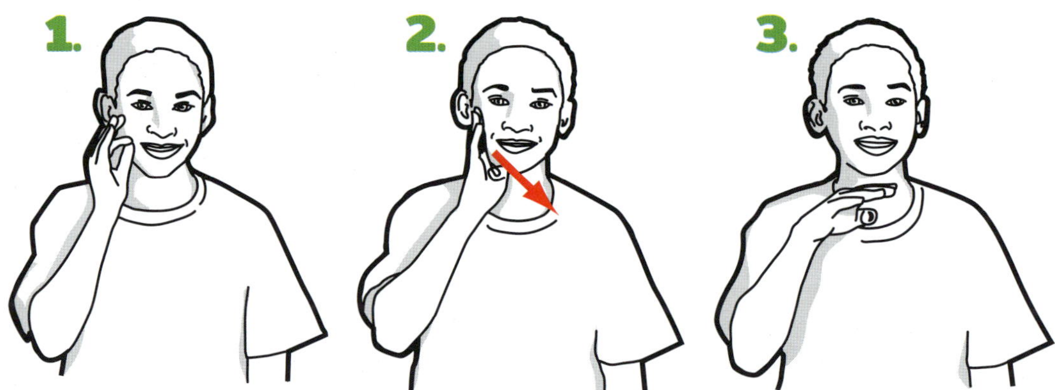

Monarch butterflies migrate to warm places for the winter.

Butterfly

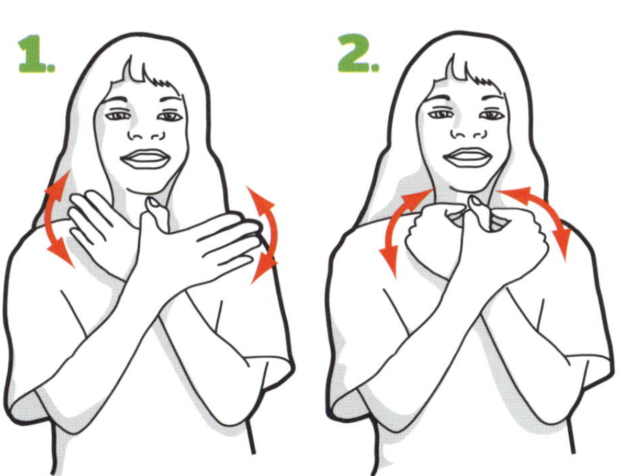

Hook your thumbs. Then flap your hands like a butterfly's wings.

Who is your favorite baseball player?

Baseball

Pretend as if you are swinging a bat.

1.

2.

What is your favorite flavor of ice cream?

Ice Cream

Make a fist and move it in front of your mouth as if you were licking an ice-cream cone.

Leaves change color in the fall.

Fall

Hold your flat left arm like a tree. Wave your flat right arm like leaves falling from the tree.

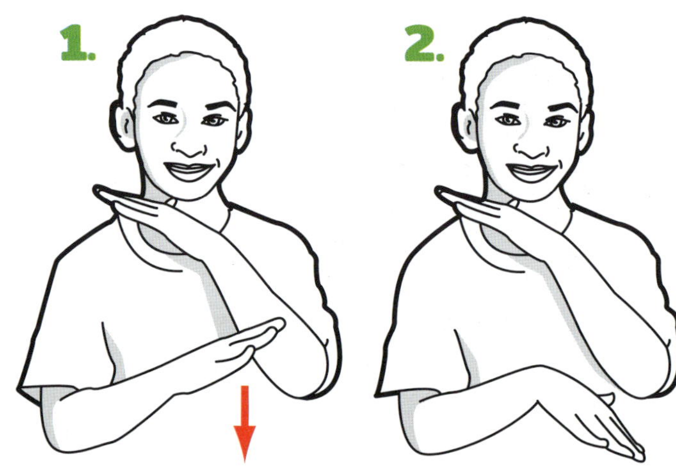

A leaf's shape depends on which type of tree it is from.

Leaf

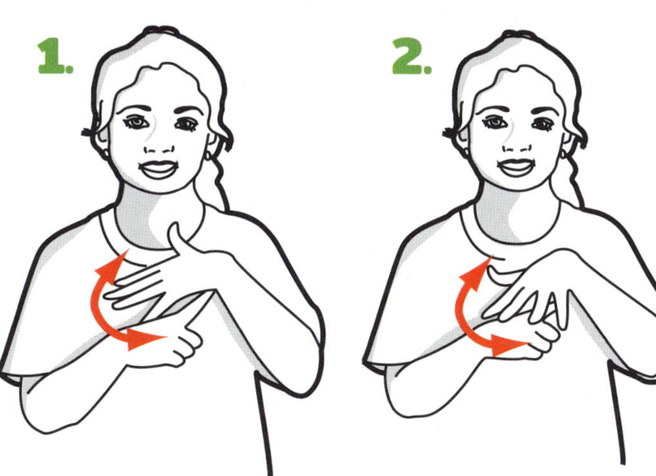

Touch your left finger to your right wrist. Wiggle your right flat hand like a leaf in the wind.

Do you have a favorite football team?

Football

Open all your fingers. Bring them together like two teams. Repeat.

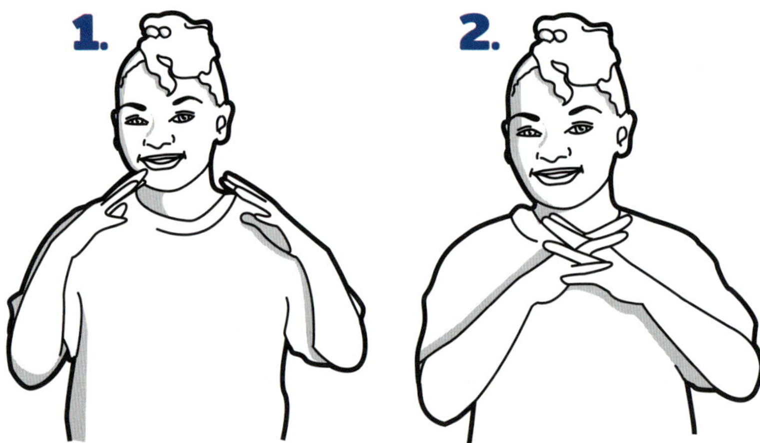

Bikes have been around for almost 200 years.

Bicycle

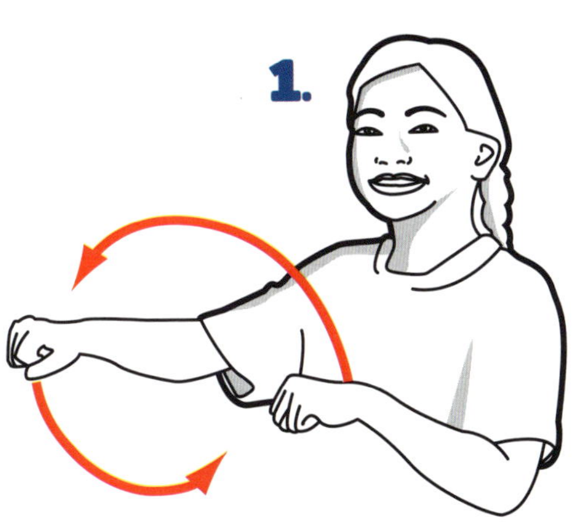

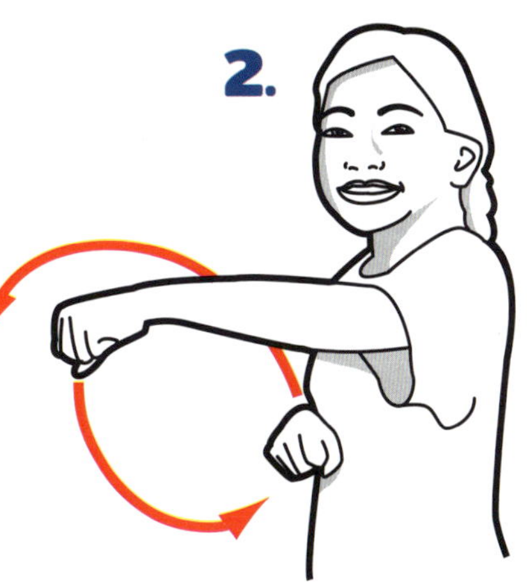

Make your hands into fists. Move them in opposite circles like pedaling a bike.

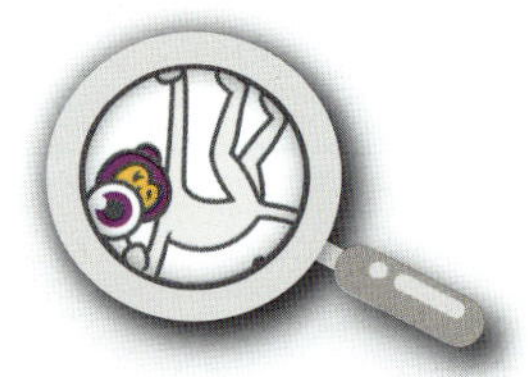

Wonder More

- How much did you know about American Sign Language (ASL) before reading this book? Do you already know some ASL signs? What new signs did you learn?

- Some words or specific names don't have signs. In these cases, you can spell the individual letters of the word, which is called fingerspelling. Look at the alphabet chart on page 23. Can you sign the letters in your name?

- With a partner, pick three signs from this book and practice them together. Are you able to understand each other? Is ASL easier or harder than you thought it would be?

- Did you know that your facial expression can affect the meaning of a sign? Why do you think our facial expressions are an important part of communication in ASL?

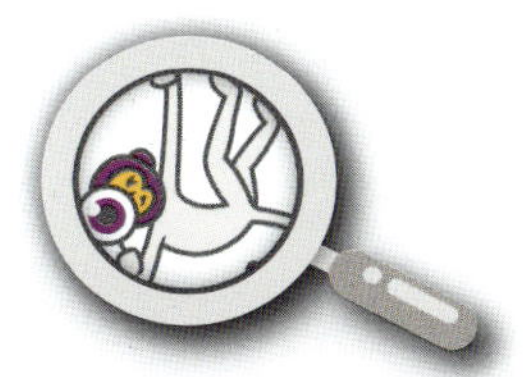

Sign Language Alphabet

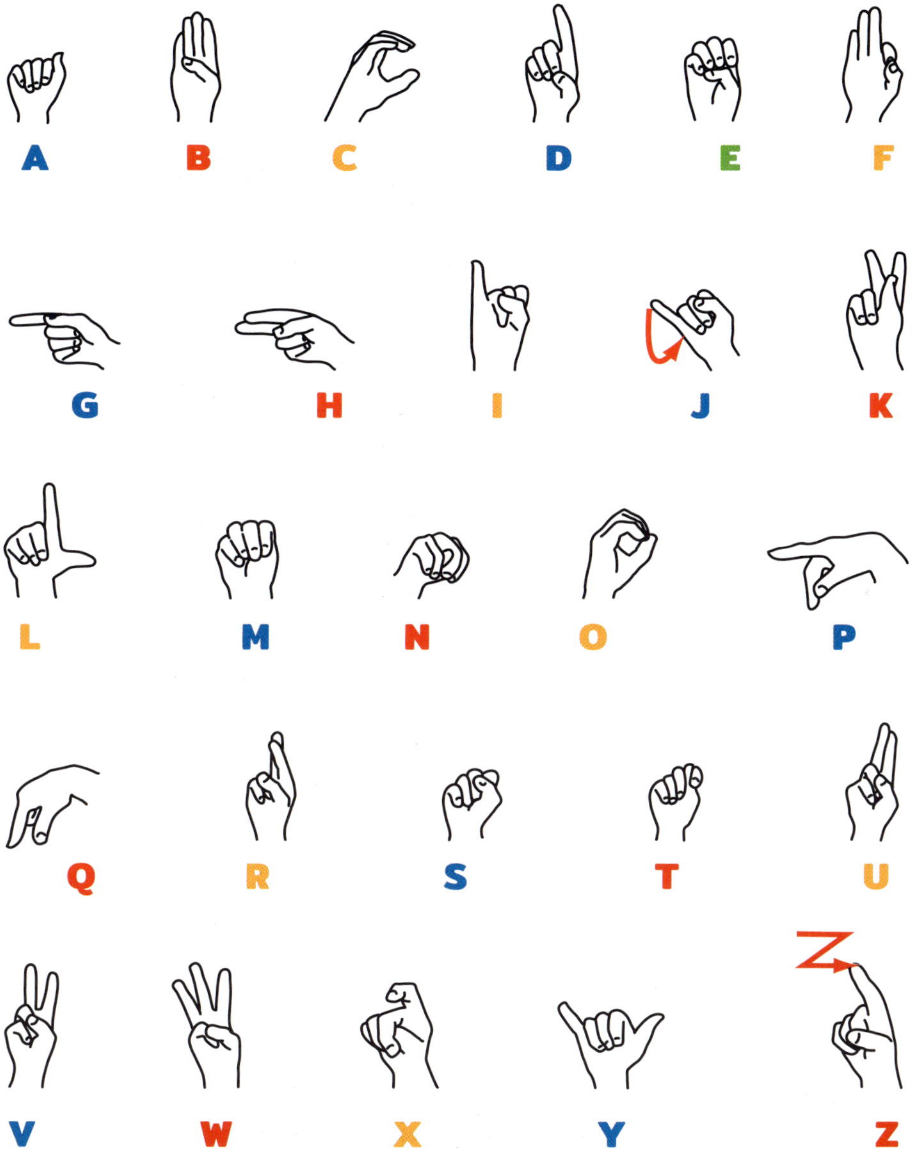

A B C D E F

G H I J K

L M N O P

Q R S T U

V W X Y Z

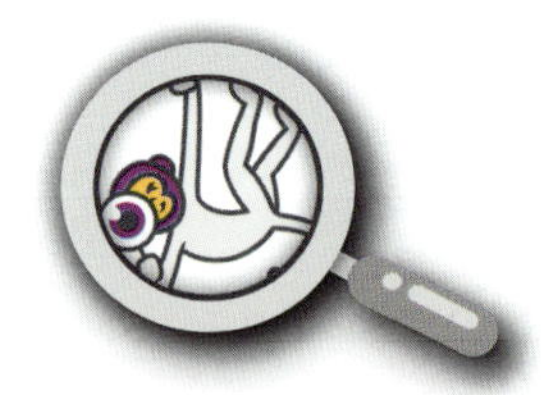

Find Out More

In the Library

Barlow, Rochelle, and Natalia Sanabria (illustrator). *American Sign Language for Kids: 101 Easy Signs for Nonverbal Communication*. Emeryville, CA: Rockridge Press, 2019.

MacLean, Roz. *More than Words: So Many Ways to Say What We Mean*. New York, NY: Henry Holt & Co., 2023.

On the Web

Visit our website for links about American Sign Language:
childsworld.com/links

Note to Parents, Caregivers, Teachers, and Librarians: We routinely verify our web links to make sure they are safe and active sites. So encourage your readers to check them out!

A Special Thank-You!

Thank you to our models from the Program for Children Who are Deaf and Hard of Hearing at the Alexander Graham Bell School in Chicago, Illinois.

Aroosa is in third grade and loves reading, shopping, and playing with her sister, Aamna. Her favorite color is red.

Carla is in fourth grade. She enjoys art and all kinds of sports.

Deandre likes playing football and watching NFL games on television. He also looks forward to going to the movies with his family.

Destiny enjoys music and dancing. She especially likes learning new things and spends much of her time practicing her cursive handwriting.

Xiomara loves fashion, clothes, and jewelry. She also enjoys music and dancing. Her favorite animal is the cat.